Byron Nelson's Winning Golf

Foreword by Tom Watson

TAYLOR PUBLISHING COMPANY
Dallas, Texas

Published by
Taylor Publishing Company
1550 West Mockingbird Lane
Dallas, Texas 75235

This is an authorized reprint of the 1946 edition of
Byron Nelson's Winning Golf.

Printed in the United States of America

10 9 8 7 6 5 4 3 2 1

Foreword
To The New Edition

When I was a young boy, my father would teach me the history of golf in the form of short stories about the great players of the game. In later years, he would quiz me on who won what and how many major championships. And then Dad would always ask me two more questions: "Who won the most tournaments in one year?" and "Who won the most tournaments in succession?" That was the first time I became aware of the golfer they called "Lord Byron."

Our friendship started in 1974 at the U.S. Open, when Byron offered solace and understanding in my time of failure. Since then, Byron has taught me more than how to hit a golf ball. . .much more. During the personal tragedy of the death of his wife Louise, I began to understand the real strength of this man, a strength that was much greater than his ability to hit the golf ball.

I've been fortunate to have witnessed Byron swing a golf club thousands of times during my many lessons from him, and I can attest to his seemingly effortless ability to hit the ball as straight as any man can hit it.

Another of Byron's great admirers, Jack Nicklaus, after attending one of Byron's 1950 golf clinics, admitted that it was the singularly most impressive ball-striking exhibition *he* had ever witnessed.

Winning Golf illustrates this timeless technique in photographs, and should be included in every golfer's library.

—TOM WATSON

DEDICATION

TO MY friends of the fairways—the membership of the Professional Golfers' Association . . .

Teaching and touring professional alike, you are aiding national welfare by encouraging myriads of men and women in all age and social categories to participate in this wonderful recreational activity.

Through hours of instruction on the practice tee, and exacting tournament competition, demonstrations, and exhibitions you are carrying to vast, improvement-hungry golfing legions the gospel of good golf.

You befriend kids who, as I did, earn their first money "packing bags." You give many of these boys their first club and instruction. You start them on the long, difficult road up so that they, too, may make their contributions to the Game.

As friend and associate you are loyal, kind, and generous. Without the encouragement and assistance received from many of you, I could never have gained the experience and knowledge which make possible WINNING GOLF.

You are the core, the life, and future of this great sport of millions.

Byron Nelson

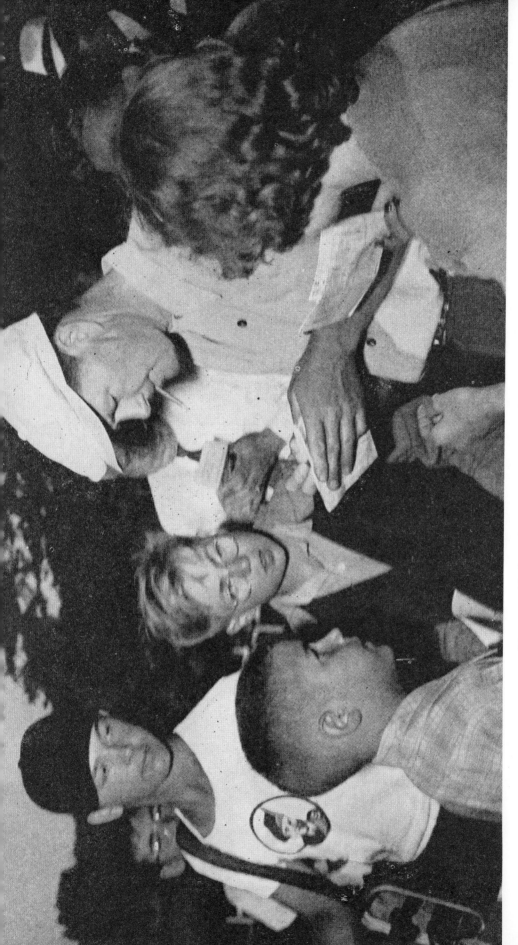

Future golf champions clamor for Byron Nelson's autograph.

FOREWORD

By Grantland Rice

ANY golf swing that carries the brilliance and consistency that Byron Nelson knows has to be sound in every detail. The continued effectiveness of Nelson's swing is proof that Byron knows at all times exactly what he is doing, and why he is doing it.

In addition to having developed a swing of this type, and this includes every shot from the drive to the putt, Nelson is also one of golf's closest and keenest students. I know of no one else who is better able to put into a golf book so much valuable instruction, information, and advice.

There are many golfers who know how to swing a club, but not so many who can scatter this information around among the millions who play and who are nearly always looking for some method to improve their play.

"I find working on this book a harder job then trying to win open tournaments," Byron wrote me. "It is far harder work than I thought it would be. My main idea is to give as clear a picture as I can of the right way to play each stroke. I want to make everything simple and direct, to keep out the confusion that so often goes with golf instruction."

Nelson's golf book, like his swing, is sound, simple, and direct. His headwork in competitive play has always been one of the features of his game, and he has certainly used his head through this book to the same extent.

WINNING GOLF is sure to be a big help to those golfers seeking to lower their scores and build upon a stronger foundation.

It goes beyond mere casual reading. It is interesting as well as instructive, coming, as it does, from one of the greatest all-around golfers, one of the greatest shot-makers who ever played through the long history of the ancient game.

Byron Nelson (right) acknowledges receipt of richest golf prize in history—$13,600 in War Bonds—for winning 1945 All-American Open tournament at Tam O'Shanter course, Chicago. Nelson won by 11 strokes with rounds of 66-68-68-67—269. Arthur Doering (left), the amateur winner, and George S. May listen attentively.

BYRON NELSON'S TOURNAMENT RECORD

MAJOR TOURNAMENTS WON

National Open Championship, 1939.

Professional Golfers' Association Match Play Championship (national) Medalist, 1937, 1940. Co-medalist, 1945. Champion, 1940, 1945.

All American Open, Tam O'Shanter Country Club, Chicago, 1941, 1942, 1944, 1945. This is world's richest meet.

Masters Tournament, Augusta, Georgia, 1937, 1942.

Western Open, 1939.

Los Angeles $10,000 Open, 1946.

Metropolitan Open, 1936.

Belmont International Match Play Championship, Belmont, Mass., 1937.

North-South Open, Pinehurst, 1939.

Hollywood (Florida) Open, 1938.

Miami $10,000 Open, 1940, 1941.

Texas Open, 1940.

Fort Worth Open, 1945.

Thomasville (Georgia) Open, 1938.

Oakland (California) Open, 1942.

San Francisco Open, 1944, 1946.

Knoxville (Tennessee) Open, 1944, 1945.

Red Cross Open, New Rochelle, N. Y., 1944.

Golden Valley Invitational, Minneapolis, 1944.

Beverly Hills (California) Open, 1944.

Nashville (Tennessee) Open, 1944.

Dallas Open, 1944.

Phoenix (Arizona) Open, 1945.

New Orleans Open, 1945, 1946.

Charlotte (North Carolina) Open, 1945.

Greensboro (North Carolina) Open, 1945.

Durham (North Carolina) Open, 1945.

Atlanta Open, 1945.

Montreal Open (Also known as Canadian P.G.A. tournament), 1945.

Philadelphia Open, 1945.

Chicago Victory Open, 1945.

Canadian Open, 1945.

Spring Lake (New Jersey) Invitational Open, 1945.

Spokane Open, 1945.

Seattle Open, 1945.

HIGHLIGHTS

Averaged 68.33 for 120 rounds of official P.G.A. tournament play during 1945 season to break his own previous all-time record of 69.67 for 85 rounds in 1944. Only golfer in history to win Radix Award with average under 71.

Set new world record for 72-hole competitive golf tournament by shooting 62-68-63-66—259 over Broadmoor course to win 1945 Seattle Open by 13 strokes.

Earned War Bonds with cash value of $52,511.32 in tournaments during 1945 season for all-time high. Broke own record of $35,005 set in 1944. Defeated Craig Wood, 1941 and "Duration-of-War" National Open champion, 15 up and 13 to play, in challenge match for unofficial world's championship at Inverness C.C., Toledo, in 1943.

Finished in money in 109 consecutive tournaments up to publication date of this book. Best previous record of 56 straight held by Ben Hogan.

Won 11 consecutive major tournaments during 1945 season for new world record. Best previous string by any golfer, 3.

Won 18 major P.G.A. sponsored tournaments in 1945 season for record. Voted "Athlete of Year" in annual Associated Press nation-wide poll, both in 1944 and 1945.

INTRODUCTION

THE *best* golf is the *easiest* golf.

Think of your own experiences on the golf course. The day the ball goes straight down the middle, and the putts are dropping, you don't work nearly as hard as when no part of your golf game is in good working order.

For further proof—look at any one of thousands of exasperated duffers as he tops, slices, hooks, dubs, and cusses his way to a 100 card. This kind of golf can't be anything else but a real mental and physical chore.

If you have ever followed a big golf tournament, you are familiar with the expression, "He makes it look easy!"—referring to a low-scoring golfer who is near or below par. It *is* easy for him, for he has learned the game properly.

To me it is incredible that so many able-bodied men and women spend so much time, energy, and money on this grand sport without ever knowing the exhilaration of playing WINNING GOLF—especially when the realization could be such a simple matter. All it takes is qualified instruction and practice.

No golfer ever gets so consistently good that he can't use some constructive advice. No matter how many trophies he may win, he can't analyze and remedy his own faults. The top men in golf know this. Unfortunately, those who need help most fail to acknowledge their deficiencies and all too seldom seek the obvious and effective remedy.

The great Bobby Jones usually had his advising professional, Stewart Maiden, readily available to "put him right," even when playing in tournaments.

One of the several reasons golf as a participant sport is so steadily expanding beyond others is its adaptability to all sizes, shapes, circumstances, and ages. It is not necessarily the tallest, strongest, youngest, most athletic, or richest who wins.

During a recent Western Amateur Tournament a youth who weighed only 100 pounds and had very limited means defeated a wealthy, strapping 6-foot 3-inch athlete. This same slight lad was a two-time amateur champion in his home state. There are in the United States today at least two one-armed golfers who shoot consistently in the 70's, or about 25 strokes under the national average.

In golf it's not who you are, what you are, or what you have that counts. It's "How badly do you *want* to win?"

If you learn to play properly—the sooner after you start, the better—you are well on your way to playing WINNING GOLF. By way of encouragement, we point out to you that golf is an exact opposite of most other sports in which complexity increases with proficiency.

As a general rule, the more you simplify and streamline your swing or stroke, the more you cut down the margin of error. It is in this respect that the greatest advances have been made in low-scoring. WINNING GOLF is based on this premise.

Byron Nelson

PREFACE

The superb golfing artistry of my friend, Byron Nelson, as he put together a particularly masterful record-breaking round inspired in me an obsession that led me to approach him soon afterward in the locker-room.

"Byron, everybody's talking about the way you hit a golf ball," I ventured, "but very few people can comprehend just how you do it. Why don't you put that golf game of yours down in black-and-white, and between covers? Tell folks in your own words just how you go about consistently shooting those incredible scores."

"Might be all right," replied the tall, wiry, affable Texan, "but what do I know about gettin' out a book. *Golf* is my business. That other is out of my line."

"Do you like the idea?" I queried. "While you do the writing I could help you with the production arrangements and other details."

"Brother, it's a deal!" exploded Byron.

WINNING GOLF was at that moment on its way. During Byron's mid-winter vacation from the tournament circuits we set to work at Fort Worth where 20 years before he played his first round of golf. Byron pitched into the project with typical drive and earnestness.

The result is before you. It's Byron Nelson's presentation and analysis of the golf game with which he has set a new world-wide standard of perfection.

—OTIS DYPWICK

ACKNOWLEDGEMENTS

To Grantland Rice for so kindly providing the Foreword.

To MacGregor Golf, Inc., for their co-operation and technical advice.

To George S. May and the George S. May Company, sponsors of the Tam O'Shanter All-American Golf tournaments, for generous contributions in factual matter and photographs.

To the Colonial Country Club, Fort Worth, Texas, for use of its course and clubhouse facilities during early production of WINNING GOLF.

To Don Bohmer for technical assistance in staging photographs.

All instructional photos by Jim Jeffreys, Camera Craft Studios, Fort Worth, Texas. Taken with speed graphic camera at 1/1000 of a second.

TABLE OF CONTENTS

CHAPTER

Chapter 1 SELECTING
YOUR EQUIPMENT

THE copious and inexpert advice most beginners receive in the matter of picking out golf clubs usually adds up to confusion and doubt in the mind of the recipient as to the most desirable quality, type, and number.

From one school of thought comes the counsel, "Get yourself any old cheap outfit to start with."

This is erroneous. Why handicap yourself with poor tools? Buy at least a medium-priced club made by a well-known, dependable manufacturer. This is your assurance of satisfaction and long wear. Buy fewer at one time, if necessary, but get good ones. They are your best long-range investment.

As to weight, length, and shaft-tension—any qualified professional can assist you in making the most prudent selection. If you live in a community where no professional is available and must thus make your own choice, select clubs that *feel* best to you—that are neither too heavy nor too light, and neither too "whippy" nor too stiff in the shaft. Generally speaking, the faster your swing, the less whip you should have in your club shafts.

Balance or distribution of weight within the club also enters the consideration, but is definitely a matter of feel.

In determining the correct length, first stand erectly, with feet spread to a width corresponding to that of your shoulders. Then bend the trunk of your body far enough forward so that your arms and hands, when hanging comfortably and loosely from the shoulders, can swing back and forth before you (past your hips) without any interference.

Next take in both hands, near the top of the club shaft (grip), a number 4 or 5 iron and rest the clubhead on the floor or ground. If the sole (bottom) of the clubhead sets flatly without having to be pushed so far away from your feet that you are reaching awkwardly, or pulled in so closely that you feel cramped, chances are the length is satisfactory. Of course, a professional can tell you in a moment whether or not your clubs fit you.

It is wise to buy "matched" irons, and "matched" woods— that is to say, clubs made by the same manufacturer, and all of the same model, weight, corresponding length, and balance. In this way you get uniformity of feel in your clubs. This is definitely desirable.

In the event you wish to buy only a bare minimum of clubs with which to start, get a driver, putter, number 3, 5, and 8 or 9 iron. The *key* clubs in learning to play golf are the number 2, 5, and 8 irons. If you learn to use these well, you will have no trouble with the others.

You will find it very much to your advantage to fill out your set as soon as possible so that you have all irons numbered 1 through 8 or 9, a putter, a sandblaster or double-duty iron, and woods numbered 1 through 4. The number 1 wood is a driver; the 2, a brassie; and woods 3 and 4, spoons. The double-duty niblick is a flanged (sole) niblick which is especially adapted to playing short pitch shots out of the edge of the rough, from sand traps, and from bunkers.

One general rule covers your choice of attire for wear while playing golf—be sure it is plenty large and loose enough. Clothes that bind or cling tightly to you hinder your swing.

Spiked shoes are preferable to any other kind. They give you the firmest foundation. These are a virtual "must," for if your feet slip or move while you are swinging, you cannot possibly hit a good shot. For the same reason, avoid loose-fitting shoes.

You will see many people wearing various types of gloves. This is a matter of individual choice. Few leading professionals use them.

An eyeshade, cap, or lightweight hat serves a highly valuable purpose in protecting your eyes from the sun on bright days.

Chapter 2 CONCENTRA-TION

CONCENTRATION, although an abstract factor in playing WINNING GOLF, belongs high on the list of essential considerations.

In the first place, it is impossible to *learn* to play golf well if you don't concentrate while undergoing instruction, whether it is written, illustrated, or personal. To profit fully, you must be both eager and intent. The benefits you derive from a study of this book will be determined by the intensity with which you concentrate on its contents, and apply the principles.

Secondly, a high degree of concentration must be invoked consistently in *playing* WINNING GOLF. This faculty is standard equipment with all champions.

Success has eluded many golfers of mechanical excellence simply because they either did not realize the importance of concentration, or had been unable to develop this power.

Golf is an exacting game—a challenge more to your mental processes than to your physical properties. The playing of *each shot* as you come to it must be uppermost in your mind. Choice of club, distances, contours, carry and roll, wind—all must be carefully considered.

It's laudable to be chatty and sociable on a golf course, but don't permit your mind to be carried off on some distant train of thought—not if you want to hit the golf ball consistently well.

You often hear the remark, "He just hasn't the temperament for golf." This is entirely possible, but frequently the individual referred to simply doesn't "think it out."

Concentration is this decisive—a player who has "all the shots" and fails to fully concentrate each time he plays one, will often lose to an opponent of inferior mechanical ability who exercises to its fullest his faculty for close mental application.

Don't let this happen to you!

Chapter 3 THE GRIP

THE grip is the most important single consideration in learning to play WINNING GOLF. The stance is next in importance.

My theory of the grip differs somewhat from that of many teachers. My grip on the club is designed for *firmness,* above all else. This is one of the real secrets of hitting a golf ball well. I grip the club very firmly in both hands, with the left hand grasping the tighter of the two.

I use what is called the "overlapping" grip. I believe this provides a maximum of coordination between hands. The effect is to make them work as one. If you have used a different type grip, you may find this one somewhat awkward at first. After you have tried it for a while, it will feel perfectly natural.

Plates 1 through 5 show you the successive steps in taking a grip on the club handle.

PLATE 1—*Placing Club in Left Hand*—Lay the club handle or grip across the index finger of the left hand as shown, with the shaft angling across the next two fingers and on up to the lower part of the palm.

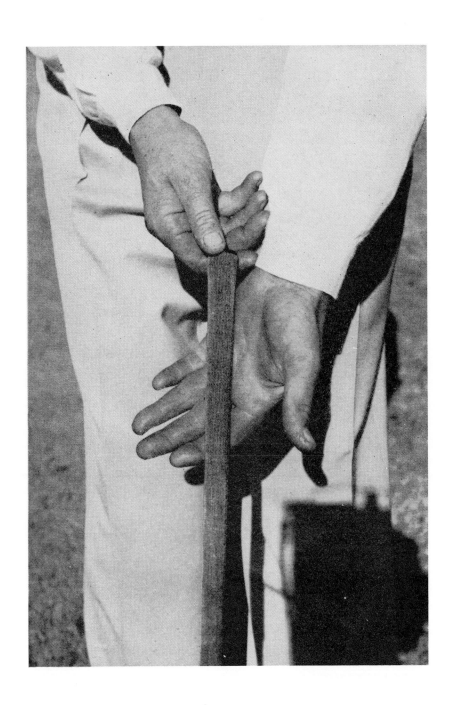

PLATE 1—*Placing Club in Left Hand*

PLATE 2—*Gripping with Left Hand*—Close the hand as shown, with the fingers firmly on the shaft handle. Note that the thumb of the left hand is closed on the shaft, a quarter of the way around. The "V" formed by the closing of the hand points approximately to the right shoulder. In looking down, you should see about half the back of your hand. Remember—the *left hand does the guiding* throughout the entire swing. At *no stage of the swing does it loosen* its grip on the club.

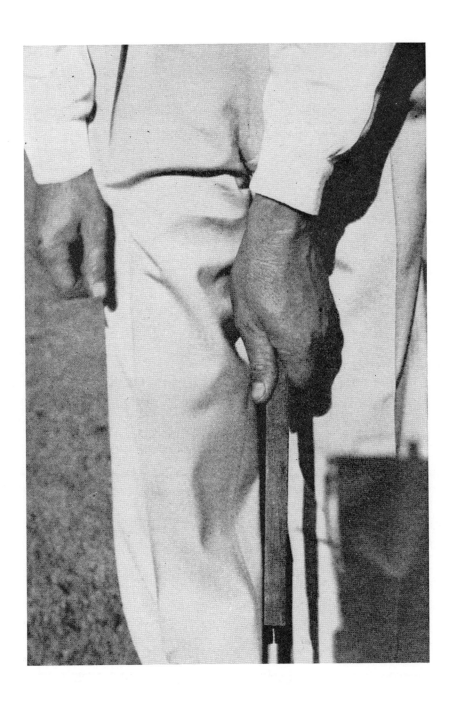

PLATE 2—*Gripping with Left Hand*

PLATE 3—*Placing Right Hand*—Place the right hand on the club as shown, with control about equally distributed between the fingers and the palm of the hand. Study this closely. It is important.

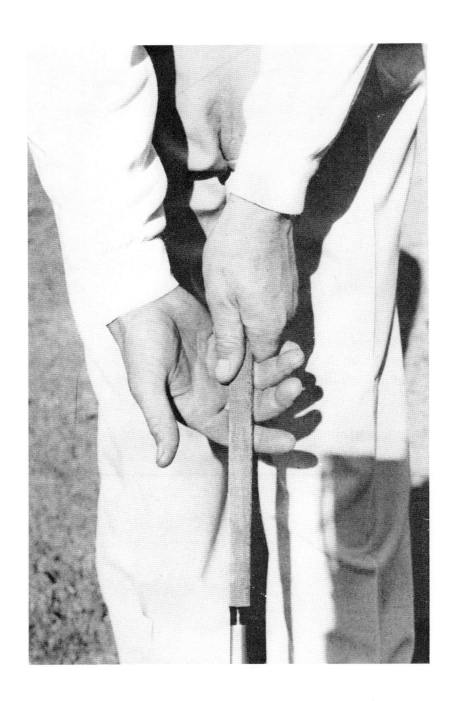

PLATE 3—*Placing Right Hand*

PLATE 4—*Position of Right Hand*—After the right hand has been closed on the club, the thumb should be one-quarter of the way around the shaft (note illustration closely) to the left. The "V" formed by the thumb and forefinger points in the general direction of the right shoulder.

The club should be gripped *firmly* by the forefinger (index finger) and the thumb of the right hand. It is in this part of your grip on the club that you get your "feel" throughout the *entire* swing.

PLATE 4—*Position of Right Hand*

PLATE 5—*Back View of Overlapping Grip*—Here you see from the back my concept of the overlapping grip. Observe that the little finger of the right hand overlaps the index finger of the left hand. Again I remind you—the last three fingers of the left hand *remain* very firmly on the club from start to finish of the swing.

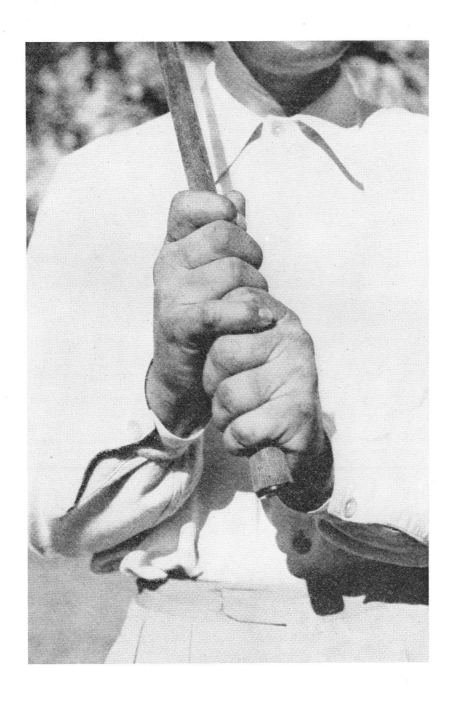

PLATE 5—*Back View of Overlapping Grip*

Chapter 4 STANCES AND ADDRESS

STANCE

"STANCE" is the position you assume in relation to the ball for playing a shot.

In taking a proper stance, you should place your feet about as far apart as the width of your shoulders, that is, for all *full* shots. Toes should always point out, which means the heels will be closer together than the toes. As an aid to accuracy, picture to yourself an imaginary line running from the spot in which you wish the ball to light back through the ball itself. This line is represented in the following photographs by the golf club on the ground.

There are three different general versions of the stance—(1) Closed, (2) Square, (3) Open.

In playing shots with *woods*, I use a *slightly closed* stance; with *long irons* (numbers 1, 2, 3), a *square* stance; with *medium irons* (numbers 4, 5, 6), a *slightly open* stance; and *short irons* (numbers 7, 8, 9), an *open* stance.

These stances vary as pictured herewith.

PLATE 6—*Closed Stance*—You will note that the right foot is pulled back from the shaft of the club on the ground which represents the line of flight to your objective. This type of stance often leads to a hooked shot (curving to the left).

PLATE 6—*Closed Stance*

PLATE *7—Square Stance*—Toes of both feet are touching the line.

PLATE 7—*Square Stance*

PLATE 8—*Open Stance*—The left foot is pulled away from the shaft, turning your body slightly toward your objective. The tendency from this stance is to slice (hit a ball that curves to the right).

PLATE 8—*Open Stance*

THE ADDRESS

When you place your clubhead down behind the ball before hitting a shot, see to it that the ball is opposite a portion of the club face (hitting surface) slightly toward the heel of the clubhead—in other words, a little back of center.

In taking position (address) for all shots you should bend over at the waist, just enough to allow the arms to hang down freely from the shoulders at a sufficient distance from the body so that there will be complete clearance for the arms and hands as they carry the club back and forward on the swing.

Never reach for the ball. Your weight as you address the ball should be *distributed evenly between the ball and the heel* of each foot, with special emphasis on the left foot. This gives you the best possible foundation for your swing.

If you start reaching perceptibly for the ball, the arc of your swing will become too flat. The predominant fault is standing too far from the ball, rather than too close to it. *It is next to impossible to stand too close* to the ball.

The Waggle. At the moment you stand ready to hit the ball there is a natural tendency to tighten up in your hands, wrists, arms, and shoulders. I have found the most effective means of overcoming this tension is the waggle—abbreviated, easy, loose, back-and-forth movement with the clubhead.

To derive maximum benefit, make these preliminary loosening-up motions in the line-of-flight in which you intend to hit the shot. The manner in which you waggle will have a definite bearing on the way you start the clubhead back for the swing. Avoid waggling too much. This defeats the purpose of the waggle.

Now, let's get on with study of the actual swing . . .

Chapter 5 UNIFORMITY OF SWING

BEFORE getting into the mechanics of the golf swing we should give attention to an important consideration—"Uniformity of Swing."

Many golfers add unnecessary complexity to the game by feeling that they must use a different swing for each club in the bag. This is incorrect.

Actually there is a slight variation in swing from club to club, *but,* you should *not make a conscious effort* to swing one club differently than another. The natural variation is caused by the different positions in which you must stand to hit the ball for the great variety of lies encountered on any course, and the range of shaft lengths and clubhead angles.

For instance, in using a driver you stand the farthest from the ball because the club shaft is longer, the clubhead at a flatter angle to the shaft, and the ball is teed up. As you use shorter clubs, move closer to the ball, and play the ball more off the center of your stance. In doing this, you automatically take a more upright and shorter swing. There is no other reason, under normal conditions, for changing your swing from shot to shot.

I am completely unaware of making any attempt to swing one club differently than another.

Chapter 6 PLAYING THE WOODS

THE DRIVER

PLATE 9—*Stance and Address*—Observe the relative position of my feet. My stance is slightly closed. I am playing the ball approximately off the left heel. Left arm and the club form a straight line from left shoulder to ball. My weight is more on the left foot than on the right. The ball should be teed approximately one inch off the ground.

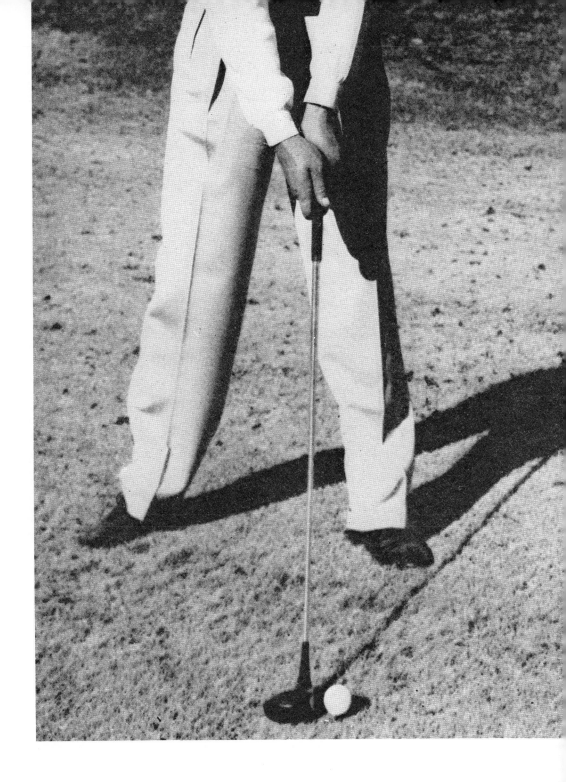

PLATE 9—*Stance and Address*

PLATE 10—*Stance and Address*—Arms are hanging from the shoulders in a comfortable position, far enough away from the body so that they can move back and forth freely throughout the entire swing. The right leg is slightly bent at the knee, causing the right shoulder to drop a little lower than the left at address. Notice that *shoulders, hips, and feet are in a parallel line with the intended flight* of the ball.

PLATE 10—*Stance and Address*

PLATE 11—*Start of Backswing*—**The clubhead, the hands, and the shoulders must start in one motion**—absolutely together. This insures a swing that is well-timed throughout its course.

The clubhead is kept low as it starts back from the ball by the shifting of weight *laterally* from the left foot to the right foot. This lateral motion causes the clubhead to travel straight back from the ball, as it should. This is important.

A grave and common error in starting the backswing is a turning motion with the hips which causes the club to cut too sharply inside as it is drawn away from the ball.

PLATE 11—*Start of Backswing*

PLATE 12—*Backswing, continued*—As you see it here, the driver has progressed on the backswing until it is approximately a quarter of the way back.

Notice that the wrists have not begun to cock. The club is being led back by the turning of the shoulders.

The weight is now shifting from the left to the right foot.

PLATE 12—*Backswing, continued*

PLATE 13—*Backswing, continued*—From this point in the backswing the hands do the work of carrying the club.

The arc of the hands is determined by the turning of the shoulders which serve the same general function as the hub in a wheel.

PLATE 13—*Backswing, continued*

PLATE 14—*Top of Backswing*—At no time make a *conscious* effort to cock the wrists. By this I am not saying that there is no cocking of the wrists. It is the deliberate attempt to do so that causes looseness in your swing—and this is a severe detriment to accuracy and consistency.

At the completion of my backswing the club is pointed at my objective (on the line of flight of the ball). My left shoulder is underneath my chin and pointing down at the ball. My left arm is *straight*.

The club is held *very* firmly by both hands at this point.

PLATE 14—*Top of Backswing*

PLATE 15—*Starting Downswing*—My first move is the beginning of transfer of weight back from my right to my left side.

I am conscious of pulling the club down with the left hip and shoulder. This leaves my hands ready to do their work as the clubhead enters the hitting zone.

Plate 15—*Starting Downswing*

PLATE 16—*Downswing, continued*—Notice that the transfer of weight from right to left is largely completed, with most of my weight now on the left foot.

Shoulders and arms are still turning and the hands are in position to release their full power at the very impact with the ball.

PLATE 16—*Downswing, continued*

PLATE 17—*Releasing Hand Power*—At the point in the swing pictured here I have the sensation of my right hand trying to catch up with my left. This is the release of power that gives your clubhead speed. The *only* way you can get maximum clubhead speed is through unleashing the full power of your hands as the clubhead enters the "hitting area"—last 20 inches before clubhead impact with ball.

Note that weight is planted firmly on the left foot.

The left hand has not turned (rolled) over, and will not do so during the entire swing. The back of the left hand is toward your objective all the time your hands are taking the clubhead into the "hitting area" and on through the early stages of the follow-through.

This method increases accuracy and consistency. It is a sure cure for the common and disastrous fault of rolling your wrists (turning the left under and the right over, as the clubhead progresses into the follow-through stage of the swing).

PLATE 17—*Releasing Hand Power*

PLATE 18—*Finish of Swing*—At the completion of the swing the power of hands, arms, and shoulders is completely spent. The club is still held *firmly*.

The center of weight distribution is on a straight line from the left foot to the top of your head.

At this point the shoulders have effected virtually a full revolution or turn from their position at the top of the backswing.

PLATE 18—*Finish of Swing*

THE BRASSIE

PLATE 19—*Stance and Swing*—The stance and swing employed in playing a brassie shot are the same as you use in playing a shot with the driver.

The principal difference is that the ball is not teed up. Because of this, you must stand slightly closer to the ball.

Note that the ball is played just a little more back toward the center of the stance than it was for a driver shot.

The swing is the same in every detail as that for the drive, even to its length.

PLATE 19—*Stance and Swing*

PLATE 20—*Position of Arms*—Notice that the arms are merely hanging—not reaching—in a free position and not too far away from the body.

Remember to start the clubhead *straight back* from the ball, and close to the ground.

To insure your doing this, *shift your weight laterally* at the hips.

Never use a brassie if you have a bad lie—one in which you cannot get a good clean sweep at the ball.

PLATE 20—*Position of Arms*

THE SPOON

The spoon is a highly important club to the average player. It is also the easiest to use. Because the clubface is lofted (tilted back) enough to get the ball well up into the air, the user seems to have more confidence in a spoon.

PLATE 21—*Position of Ball*—You will notice that the ball is still farther back of the left heel (more toward the center of the stance) for a spoon shot than for the brassie and driver.

As you can see, the left arm and club shaft form virtually a straight line. The hands are ahead of the clubhead and ball.

The weight is balanced toward the left side.

PLATE 21—*Position of Ball*

PLATE 22—*Stance*—The stance is still slightly closed (right foot back from the line of flight more than the left).

The arms are hanging in a free, natural position, with the hands close to the body.

There is a slight bend at the waist.

PLATE 22—*Stance*

PLATE 23—*Start of Backswing*—Again, as with the other woods, the clubhead is coming straight back from the ball.

There is no rolling of the wrists. The *back of my left hand is squarely toward the objective,* and the back of the right is squarely away from the objective.

The clubhead is travelling low along the ground.

PLATE 23—*Start of Backswing*

PLATE 24—*Shifting of Weight*—At the stage of the back-swing illustrated here you can see that the weight is shifting well back to the right side.

The left shoulder is beginning to turn underneath the chin.

The left arm is still *straight*. There has been no cocking of the wrists.

PLATE 24—*Shifting of Weight*

PLATE 25—*Starting Clubhead Back*—This is virtually the same position as that illustrated in Plate 24, but from the front.

The slight bend in the shaft makes it apparent that the clubhead is picking up some speed on its backward journey. You must be careful not to start the clubhead back too fast. If you do, your swing is certain to be too loose, and you will expend all your power before you hit the ball.

Club and left arm are still in a straight line.

My head is directly over the ball. It remains in this position throughout the swing.

PLATE 25—*Starting Clubhead Back*

PLATE 26—*Top of Backswing*—This illustration catches the precise top of the backswing.

Note the straightness of the left arm.

My weight is planted securely on the right foot and leg.

The club is pointing toward the intended flight of the ball.

My hands are very *firmly* on the club, with the grip of the last three fingers on the left hand being especially solid.

The right elbow and right arm are fairly close to the right side, but *not clamped* down.

My shoulders have completed a half-arc, and the back of my shoulders is nearly square toward the objective.

PLATE 26—*Top of Backswing*

PLATE 27—*Start of Downswing*—One of the most prevalent errors is the practice of starting the club down from the top of the backswing with the hands. *This is wrong.*

At the point in the swing illustrated here, the *left shoulder* and *left side* have begun to pull the club down into hitting position.

The hands are still leading the clubhead.

Weight has shifted to the extent that it is planted solidly on both feet.

PLATE 27—*Start of Downswing*

PLATE 28—*Downswing, continued*—At this point the down-swing has progressed more than halfway.

The preponderance of weight has shifted to the left side, particularly to the left heel. The right heel is beginning to rise slightly.

The left arm and left shoulder are still pulling the club in its arc toward the ball.

The hands have not begun to unleash their power, being in readiness to do so as the clubhead enters the hitting area toward the bottom of the arc.

PLATE 28—*Downswing, continued*

PLATE 29—*Finishing Swing*—Always remember that your **swing does not end at clubhead impact** with the ball. You must hit *completely through*. The ball is hit from impact on *through*, and not *to* the ball. This holds true for all clubs.

My hands are still firmly in control of the club at finish of the swing.

The back of my shoulders is in exactly the opposite position from what it was at the top of the backswing.

My weight is planted completely and firmly on my left foot.

My head is still in the same position in relation to my body and stance as it was at the address of the ball, but has turned, permitting my eyes to follow the flight of the ball. This motion is entirely natural, and coordinated with the turning of the shoulders.

The supposition that the eyes must remain fixed throughout the follow-through on the spot from which the ball was hit is completely erroneous. This is unnatural and retards the free and full turn of the shoulders to the point shown in Plate 29.

PLATE 29—*Finishing Swing*

Chapter 7 PLAYING THE LONG IRONS

ONE important fact to keep in your mind as we consider the technique of playing shots with the long irons (numbers 1 through 3) is that the ball is struck a *descending* blow. In other words, the bottom of the arc of the swing comes slightly forward of the position in which the ball lies.

This means that the sole of the blade or clubhead cuts down into the turf *after* initial clubface impact with the ball.

It is especially important that the face of your club be at right angles (square) to the line of flight for all normal shots.

PLATE 30—*Stance for Long Iron*—Left arm and the club form a straight line from shoulder to ball.

The weight is planted firmly on both feet, with perhaps a slight bit more on the left.

The "V" formed by the grip of both hands is pointing in the direction of the right shoulder.

The ball is played nearly directly out from the left heel.

The head is in a position above the ball so that you can easily see the ball out of the left eye.

The right shoulder is somewhat lower than the left. This is caused by the slight relaxing of the right leg at the knee. This allows the right hip and shoulder to drop down into the position shown and places weight emphasis on left foot.

Again I remind you—to hit iron shots firmly you must always have a firm grip on the club *throughout* the swing.

PLATE 30—*Stance for Long Iron*

PLATE 31—*Stance, continued*—The stance, as shown, is square. Feet are equi-distant from the imaginary line of flight.

The hands are close to the body, thus assuring an upright arc in the swing.

The arms are hanging in a free position—not reaching for the ball. The body is slightly bent at the waist.

If you start the clubhead away from the ball correctly, it's almost impossible to swing incorrectly. Most mistakes are made at the address and in starting the club on the backswing. Of course you can offset mistakes in swing by proper use of hands at the bottom of the swing, but this takes an experienced player, and a man with exceptionally good feel in his hands.

PLATE 31—*Stance, continued*

PLATE 32—*Start of Backswing*—Note that the clubhead is being taken back low along the ground.

Hands, clubhead, and left shoulder have started to move simultaneously. At this point weight is beginning to shift laterally from left to right.

PLATE 32—*Start of Backswing*

PLATE 33—*Backswing, continued*—The clubhead is now beginning to take a more upright course in its backward arc,
carried by the hands through the turning of the shoulders, and
the shifting of weight from left to right.

The clubhead is beginning to come slightly "inside" (the line
of flight).

PLATE 33—*Backswing, continued*

PLATE 34—*Backswing, continued*—The clubhead is now near the halfway mark in the backswing.

The right leg is straight. The left leg is bent slightly, with the weight shifting toward the right.

The left arm and the club form nearly a straight line. The right elbow is fairly close to the right side, but isn't crowding it.

The shoulders are nearing a full turn.

PLATE 34—*Backswing, continued*

PLATE 35—*Top of Backswing*—**Both hands are firmly in control of the club.** The shoulders have revolved until they are facing squarely toward the objective.

Left arm is straight, and the left shoulder has come around under the chin. The head is not quite directly over the ball.

The center of balance is toward the heel of the *right* foot.

The way to assure good timing in your swing is to slow down your backswing, even to a point of slight hesitation at the top. Motion of body, arms, hands, and club must all stop at top before downswing is started.

PLATE 35—*Top of Backswing*

PLATE 36—*Maximum Backswing*—I have purposely taken the clubhead farther back than I normally do in playing an iron shot.

My purpose is to show you the maximum distance I believe a club may be taken back without over-swinging. My hands are at a maximum height. I do not advocate going back this far, but do not say it is wrong.

If you swing back *beyond* this point, any or all of the three following errors will occur:

1. Your head will have to move out of position.
2. Your left arm will have to bend.
3. Your grip on the club will loosen.

Any one of these three mistakes is enough to result in a poorly hit shot.

I believe that a person swinging the club back this far, and no farther, may obtain maximum distance and accuracy. However, this is a borderline case. There is nothing to be gained by this excess.

Any time you over-swing, you become inaccurate.

PLATE 36—*Maximum Backswing*

PLATE 37—*Start of Downswing*—The clubhead starts down
with the shifting of weight back to the left side. Coordinated
with this motion is the pulling effect of the left shoulder as it
begins to turn, and the sliding of the left hip back to its original
position.

These combined motions pull the hands down, causing them
to gather momentum. Note closely—the wrists and hands have
not even begun to unleash their power. They are *ready*.

PLATE 37—*Start of Downswing*

PLATE 38—*Downswing, continued*—The clubhead has reached approximately the halfway mark in the downswing, but the *hands are still cocked.* None of their power has been expended as yet.

Weight has been transferred well over to the left side.

The right shoulder is slightly lower than the left.

The right knee is somewhat bent, causing the right heel to raise just a little off the ground.

At this point in the swing, your hands are ready to uncoil soon with maximum speed and strength.

PLATE 38—*Downswing, continued*

PLATE 39—*Entering Hitting Area*—Notice that the head is well back of the ball.

The weight has clearly shifted to the left side.

The hands are releasing the power that must be turned on to give the clubhead maximum speed. To me it seems that my right hand is trying to catch up with my left which is pulling the club through at high speed.

The back of the left hand faces the objective.

PLATE 39—*Entering Hitting Area*

PLATE 40—*Finish of Swing*—You will notice in this photo that the finishes of all swings are similar.

Of course, the hands finish a little higher when playing the long irons, as compared to the woods, because the swing is more upright.

The weight is planted on the left foot, with balance toward the heel.

The club is still gripped very firmly.

Note that the head has turned toward the objective, permitting the eyes to follow the ball. You must be careful that the head does not turn before this point: when the clubhead has gone as far through on the line of flight as possible, before turning inward and upward in its arc. As the right shoulder passes under the chin, it is natural for the head to start turning with the shoulders and the pull of the arms as they continue through to the end of the swing.

Again I remind you—always hit all the way through with your shot. Let hands and clubhead follow after the ball. Keep your head back of the ball.

PLATE 40—*Finish of Swing*

Chapter 8 PLAYING THE MEDIUM IRONS

PLATE 41—*Stance and Address (Front)*—Note that the feet are a little closer together for the medium irons (numbers 4, 5, 6) than in the stance for longer shots.

The ball is played from approximately the center of the stance.

The hands are ahead of the clubhead. The arm and club form nearly a straight line from the left shoulder to the ball.

PLATE 41—*Stance and Address (Front)*

PLATE 42—*Stance and Address (Side, Rear)*—In observing the position of the feet you see that the stance for playing medium irons is *slightly open*.

My body is fairly erect, with a slight bend at the waist.

The hands are quite close to the body.

Because the club shaft is shorter and the angle of the head more upright, I stand closer to the ball than for a shot with a long iron.

The weight is more on the left foot, with the right knee bent slightly. This brings the right shoulder down a little lower than the left.

PLATE 42—*Stance and Address (Side, Rear)*

PLATE 43—*Start of Backswing*—The clubhead starts on an upright course sooner than in playing a longer iron. This is caused by the fact that the feet are closer together than in the stance for a longer iron; and the body is a little more upright. The natural consequence is for the clubhead to describe a more upright arc.

PLATE 43—*Start of Backswing*

PLATE 44—*Backswing, continued*—Notice particularly that the left arm and club shaft still form virtually a straight line. The wrists have not begun to cock.

The club has been carried to this position through the turning of the shoulders, and the *lateral shifting* of the hips.

Transfer of weight to the right foot is well under way.

PLATE 44—*Backswing, continued*

PLATE 45—*Backswing, continued*—As the clubhead nears the top of the backswing the *left arm is still straight,* as always. The right arm is fairly close to the side.

The head is nearly over the ball.

The left shoulder is turning under the chin.

Weight has shifted largely to the right side.

PLATE 45—*Backswing, continued*

PLATE 46—*Top of Backswing*—This backswing is not as long as that used in playing a long iron.

The accuracy factor becomes greater and the distance factor less as we decrease the range of the clubs.

Notice that the left arm is *still straight*.

The shoulders have made a half turn with back of them toward the objective.

Hips and weight have not shifted as much to the right as they do in playing longer shots.

The left heel is only slightly off the ground. This is an aid to hitting *down* and *through* the ball—a necessity in putting backspin on the ball.

If all the weight had been transferred to the right foot as for the longer full shots, the clubhead would sweep the ball off the turf and hit it too high. There would be no backspin.

PLATE 46—*Top of Backswing*

PLATE 47—*Downswing*—At the point in the downswing illustrated here, the clubhead is half way down.

The weight is firmly planted on *both* feet.

The left shoulder and side are firmly set, so that the hands can hit *through* on the shot and keep the club straight on the line.

PLATE 47—*Downswing*

PLATE 48—*Downswing, continued*—Weight is well on to the left side now.

Hands and club are about to enter the hitting area.

Wrists are still unspent and ready to impart the full final burst of speed and power to the club for impact with the ball.

PLATE 48—*Downswing, continued*

PLATE 49—*Entering Hitting Area*—At the point in the downswing illustrated here, the clubhead and hands are entering the hitting area.

The left hand and arm are still *pulling* the clubhead, with the right hand trying to catch up. It is this action which gives you the full clubhead speed.

You can see that the clubhead is travelling down. This means that the club is going to strike the ball a downward blow, pinching the ball against the turf and imparting backspin to it.

Remember this—if in playing this shot you had too much weight on the right foot, chances are you would hit up on the ball, rather than down. The result would be a ball with too high a flight, or else a "topped" ball.

PLATE 49—*Entering Hitting Area*

PLATE 50—*Point of Impact*—Give particular attention to the position of the hands in this illustration. The ball has been struck and the clubhead is cutting through the turf—the first stage of the follow-through.

The *back of the left hand has not turned over or away.* It is still directly toward the hole.

The right hand has completely caught up with the left at this point and has expended the power which imparts clubhead speed.

Notice that the arms are close to the body.

The head has not moved out of position.

Weight is well on to the left foot.

Check this illustration with number 39. You will see that you do not use as much body in playing the medium irons as for the long irons.

From this position the **hands follow the clubhead and the ball straight out to the full extension of the arms.** Then the hands and clubhead begin to come up and around the shoulders.

PLATE 50—*Point of Impact*

PLATE 51—*Finish of Swing*—In studying this finish of the swing you will see that it is necessary to swing completely through on *every* shot, regardless of how short the backswing may have been. THIS IS IMPORTANT!

The hands are still firmly on the club and very much in control, as they were all the way through the swing.

The shoulders have made a full turn from the top of the backswing.

The weight is principally on the left foot.

The head has followed the turn of the shoulders in the final stages of the follow-through, permitting the eyes to follow the ball.

PLATE 51—*Finish of Swing*

Chapter 9 PLAYING THE SHORT IRONS

Pₗₐₜₑ 52—*Stance and Address*—In studying this photo, note the following points:

When using the short irons (numbers 7, 8, 9) the ball is to be played from opposite a point approximately halfway between the left and right feet, or, as it is called, "the center of the stance."

The feet are closer together than for the medium irons.

The left arm and the club still form a straight line, as in playing all other shots.

The weight is slightly over to the left side.

PLATE 52—*Stance and Address*

PLATE 53—*Stance and Address, continued*—You can see that the stance is open.

Hands are very close to the body. The club is gripped about an inch and a half from the end of the shaft.

Inasmuch as the club is shorter than those we have been studying, it is necessary to bend over a little more at the waist. My eyes are very nearly directly over the ball.

The reason for gripping the club a little shorter is that this practice helps assure a good grip and better "feel" of the clubhead. *Accuracy* is the prime essential of a short iron shot. This added control and feel are important in achieving accuracy.

You should not try to use one of these irons for a shot of more than 125 yards.

PLATE 53—*Stance and Address, continued*

PLATE 54—*Start of Backswing*—The clubhead is started back on a more upright arc than in execution of shots previously considered. The reasons are that you are (1) bent over a little more, (2) gripping the club a little shorter.

The weight has shifted slightly to the right foot.

The shoulders are turning in unison with the upsweep of the hands and assisting in the lifting.

PLATE 54—*Start of Backswing*

PLATE 55—*Backswing*—The club has reached the three-quarters mark in the backswing for a short iron.

The wrists have cocked considerably more than they do in playing a longer iron. The reason—for short shots you hit the ball more with the hands and arms.

PLATE 55—*Backswing*

PLATE 56—*Top of Backswing*—Notice especially that the club has been swung into quite an upright position.

The club has been kept well on the line.

The left arm is still straight.

The weight has moved only slightly to the right side.

There has been very litle hip movement.

The shoulders have turned considerably, illustrating the point that **the club is carried by the shoulders and arms.**

The head is in a steady position, directly over the ball.

PLATE 56—*Top of Backswing*

PLATE 57—*Downswing*—The clubhead has travelled about halfway down to the point of impact with the ball.

Already the weight is well back on to the left side.

The head has remained motionless.

The left arm is perfectly straight, and the right arm is close to the side.

Wrists are still cocked, holding in reserve their full power which is to reach maximum peak at point of impact.

PLATE 57—*Downswing*

PLATE 58—*Downswing, continued*—With the clubhead about to contact the ball, the head is still in position.

Weight has shifted to the left side.

The left hand is pulling as the right hand tries to catch up with it. ***The wrists are nearly fully uncocked. Back of left hand is still squarely toward the objective.***

The clubhead is about to strike the ball a *descending* blow. This will pinch the ball against the turf and the face of the club, imparting tremendous backspin to the ball.

PLATE 58—*Downswing, continued*

PLATE 59—*Finish of Swing*—Notice that the follow-through in playing a short iron is not as long as that employed in the longer shots. However, the clubhead and hands have travelled all the way through on the shot. They *must not quit early,* just because the shot is shorter.

The follow-through must be long enough to assure transfer of your weight fully to the left side, thereby enabling your hands and club to follow through completely *on line.*

PLATE 59—*Finish of Swing*

Chapter 10 PITCH AND CHIP SHOTS

THE pitch shots and chip shots are tremendously important scoring factors. To me they are the most valuable shots in anyone's game.

I am frequently asked, "When do you pitch the ball, and When do you chip it?"

To this I answer, "I pitch the ball whenever possible because there are no hazards in the air. A ball that is chipped may bounce off line, thereby spoiling its accuracy"

THE PITCH SHOT

In the situation pictured in the following illustration, I am set to pitch to a green from a point about 15 yards off the edge of the green.

PLATE 60—*Stance and Address*—You will notice in studying this illustration that the ball is played with the club face at loft or "open."

The ball is directly out from a point halfway between the feet.

The club is gripped short (down from the top of the shaft).

Note that the feet are close together.

PLATE 60—*Stance and Address*

PLATE 61—*Stance and Address, continued*—Hands are very close to the body. The bend of the body at the waist drops the hands down nearly to the knees.

Stance is quite open, enabling you to hit *through the ball* right on the line of flight, and with freedom.

The swing from this point is identical to that described under "Playing the Short Irons."

Be sure in playing this shot not to use much body.

Be careful to transfer your weight on a limited basis.

This shot is played primarily by the hands and arms. Both hands must be *firm* throughout, as in all other shots.

You must keep your head and body comparatively still. Obviously, some motion of the feet, hips, and shoulders is necessary. The shoulders must move with the hands and arms.

For this shot you do not start the clubhead back close to the ground. You *pick it up fairly sharply* on the backswing. This places the clubhead in position to strike the ball a sharp downward blow. This blow causes the backspin so necessary to making the ball stop abruptly after landing.

To assure backspin, keep your *weight on the left foot* and allow the *forefinger and thumb of the right hand* to play an active part in the swinging of the club. This leads to the little additional wrist action which tends to bring the clubhead up at a sharper angle on the backswing. The desired descending blow follows, producing the backspin.

A ball pitched on to the green with no backspin may roll across the green and into trouble—possibly a sand trap.

In playing this shot be sure to keep your left hand especially firm on the club, and in control.

It is just as necessary to stroke and *hit through* on this shot as any of the others we have studied. As stated in the chapter "Playing the Short Irons," the follow-through is not as extended as for the longer irons. But, again I say, remember to hit through the ball and toward the hole.

PLATE 61—*Stance and Address, continued*

THE CHIP SHOT

PLATE 62—*Stance and Address*—The chip shot (or pitch-and-run, as some people call it) is played with a rather relaxed grip.

As you can see in the illustration, the ball is approximately off the middle of the stance.

The feet are quite close together, with weight about evenly distributed.

The arms hang rather loosely, and very close to the body.

I am standing fairly erectly.   (See Plate 63.)

PLATE 62—*Stance and Address*

PLATE 63—*Stance, Address, Generalities*—The stance is slightly open.

Because of the relaxed state of the hands and arms in playing this shot, the clubhead travels *low along the ground—both* on the *backswing* and the *follow-through.*

You *must* carry your clubhead *straight back* on the line of flight, and stroke it straight through on the line of flight (toward the hole).

This low, straight motion imparts overspin to the ball, and makes it roll true.

This shot is usually played from only a few yards off the green, and where the terrain between the ball and green is fairly level.

The most effective clubs are the number 4 or number 5 iron.

PLATE 63—*Stance, Address, Generalities*

Chapter 11 PUTTING

THERE are many styles and methods of putting that have proven effective over a space of time. Several are extreme.

In my opinion, putting is a matter of *feel* and *concentration*. It is important, regardless of the grip you employ, that your hands *work together as one*.

My putting grip varies somewhat from the conventional, but has proven effective.

PLATE 64—*Placing Left Hand*—First I take the club handle in the middle finger of the left hand, letting it extend diagonally across the palm as illustrated. Note very closely the angle at which the shaft comes up across the palm.

The index finger is pointing down.

PLATE 64—*Placing Left Hand*

PLATE 65—*Placing Right Hand*—Now I slide the *third finger* of the right hand up against the *middle finger* of the left hand, allowing the *little finger* of the right hand to *overlap* the middle finger of the left hand.

I have the putter in the *first three fingers* of the *right hand,* and the *last three fingers* of the left hand.

PLATE 65—*Placing Right Hand*

PLATE 66—*Placing Left Thumb*—I keep the *left thumb* straight down the top of the shaft (note closely), and dig the end of the right thumb and fingernail down into the top of the shaft, as shown.

The *index finger* of the *left hand* lies easily across the *first three fingers* of the *right hand*.

PLATE 66—*Placing Left Thumb*

PLATE 67—*Back View of Grip*—The club is now held very firmly in the three gripping fingers of the left hand.

The *feel* of the putter head comes from the forefinger and thumb of the right hand.

My reason for pinching the end of the thumb of the right hand in to the top of the shaft is that I have found it much easier to **in this manner keep the face of the club square with the line** to the hole. It eliminates the turning, open or closed, of the face of the putter.

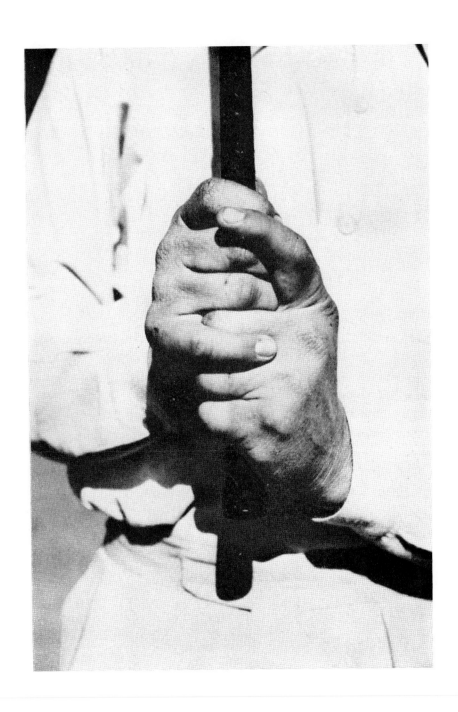

PLATE 67—*Back View of Grip*

PLATE 68—*Stance and Address*—I play the ball approximately off the left heel, as shown.

Notice that my hands are slightly ahead of the ball and clubhead.

My right elbow is resting on the right hip.

My left elbow is bent, and points off to the left.

The *unified motion* of my hands is such that the clubhead is carried back *low and on line,* and *follows through low and on line.*

In stroking the longer putts, the right elbow slides off my right hip in a line toward the cup after the putter blade has struck the ball. This permits the follow-through necessary in playing a long putt.

PLATE 68—*Stance and Address*

PLATE 69—*Stance and Address, continued*—The right elbow is shown clearly here, resting lightly on the right hip.

The putter *blade is square to the hole,* and the stance is slightly open.

Bend enough to have your eyes directly over the ball.

Of great importance in putting well is keeping both head and body completely still throughout the entire stroke.

PLATE 69—*Stance and Address, continued*

Chapter 12 SAND TRAP SHOTS

THERE is greater tolerance in playing out of a sand trap than for any other shot in the game.

It is possible to hit one, two or even three inches behind the ball as it rests in the sand, and still get it out on to the green.

The most prevalent mistake by the average golfer is in taking too short a swing, and failing to hit all the way through. Remember, this shot is *always* played with a *full swing*. It is fatal to hit into the sand and not follow through.

The *length of the flight of the ball* is determined by the *distance you hit behind the ball*. For the maximum distance which should be sought with the number 9 iron, sandblaster, or double duty niblick in playing from sand, you should hit approximately one-half inch behind the ball. The shorter the distance desired, the more you hit behind the ball.

If you cut down into the sand a half inch below the ball, you are taking plenty of sand. Do not go any deeper, unless the ball is buried. In this event, you may have to take more sand. If the ball is buried, be sure to plant your feet solidly enough so that you do not slip out of position. A slip may cause you to miss the shot.

PLATE 70—*Playing a Normal Trap Shot*—Plant your feet firmly in the sand.

Play the ball from a point approximately off the left heel.

Note that the clubface is open (laid back).

The left arm and the club form a straight line extending from the shoulder to the ball.

The distance you must aim to hit behind the ball in playing a normal trap shot from loose sand is two inches.

I am using a double duty-niblick.

PLATE 70—*Playing a Normal Trap Shot*

PLATE 71—*Stance and Address; Start of Backswing*—The stance should be quite open, thus allowing you to take the club-head up and back outside the line of intended flight. The purpose is to enable you to cut across the ball from outside to inside as you hit it. This action causes the ball to rise sharply.

PLATE 71—*Stance and Address; Start of Backswing*

PLATE *72—Backswing—*The weight is shifting from the left to the right.

The shoulders are turning.

The club is in an upright position.

The wrists are almost fully cocked.

PLATE 72—*Backswing*

PLATE *73—Top of Backswing*—Note closely the following points:
Wrists are fully cocked.
Head is directly over the ball.
The weight has transferred well to the right side.
Shoulders have made a half turn.
Left arm is still straight.

PLATE 73—*Top of Backswing*

PLATE 74—*Downswing*—At the point in the downswing illustrated here the weight has moyed well back on to the left side.

The wrists are still cocked.

The shoulders are turning.

The left arm is pulling down, furnishing enough power to enable you to hit completely through on the shot.

PLATE 74—*Downswing*

PLATE 75 — *End of Swing* — Notice that there has been a complete follow-through on the shot.

Weight is balanced completely on the left foot.

Shoulders have completed a full turn from their position at the top of the backswing. The head has turned with them from the point in the follow-through at which the club is pointing directly at your objective, permitting the eyes to follow the flight of the ball.

Hands are still *firmly on the club,* and in *full control.*

PLATE 75 — *End of Swing*

Chapter 13 VARIATIONS

T HERE are instances in which, because of obstacles or hazards, it is necessary to hit a ball either higher or lower than
you normally would with a given club. A low-flying ball will
come in handy when strong winds prevail. Or, you may find it
desirable to curve the ball around a barrier.

You must then make adjustments in your stance and swing
to bring about an abnormal result.

I do not advise your trying to work out these variations while
you are in the elementary stages of learning golf. You must
first master the fundamentals, and then develop an all-around
sound mastery of strokes before delving into the more intricate
details involved in purposely hitting a ball high, low, or with
a curve.

HITTING THE BALL HIGH

PLATE 76—*Stance, Address for High Shot*—In this instance
I am using a number 7 iron. The ball is being played from a
point approximately opposite the left heel.

The hands are even with the clubhead, and not ahead of it
as in playing all normal shots.

The weight is planted more on the *right* foot than on the left.
When you hit the ball from this position, with the hands slightly
behind the clubhead, you will catch the ball on the *upswing*. This
means an abnormally high trajectory. It holds true, regardless
of the club used.

PLATE 76—*Stance, Address for High Shot*

PLATE *77—Downswing*—Even with the clubhead entering the hitting area, my weight is still planted on *both* feet, with only a slight shift to the left side.

The wrists have uncocked a little earlier than they would in playing a normal shot, the purpose being to bring the clubhead into the ball slightly on the upswing. This technique results in more height to the flight of the ball.

PLATE 77—*Downswing*

HITTING THE BALL LOW

PLATE 78—*Stance and Address*—To hit the ball low, you actually reverse the procedure for hitting it high.

The ball is played from a point approximately off the right foot, with the hands unusually far ahead of the clubhead (as pictured).

The stance is slightly open.

Note the straight line formed by the left arm and the club from the left shoulder to the ball.

Weight is planted very firmly on the left foot, and the balance of weight does not leave this foot at any stage of the swing. This contributes to an upright backswing.

Be sure to keep a very firm grip on the club with the *left* hand. This prevents any possible turning of the clubhead at the point of impact with the ball.

In playing this shot you do not employ as long a backswing or follow-through as for a normal shot. The reason—you must have extra firmness in the left hand, arm, and side. In keeping the weight preponderantly on the left foot, you automatically retard the backswing, thereby cutting down its length.

PLATE 78—*Stance and Address*

PLATE *79—Downswing*—You will note that the weight has moved extraordinarily far ahead of the ball (compare with Plate *77*).

The hips have moved forward beyond the ball.

At this point in the swing, the left arm is still pulling the clubhead.

The wrists will uncock late, causing the clubhead to strike the ball decidedly on the downswing. The effect is to pinch the ball between the clubface and the turf, causing it to travel on a low trajectory throughout its flight.

Be very sure to keep the left arm and hand firmly in position. If you permit them to turn over, you will cause a pronounced hook.

A shot that causes the ball to travel low is a strong asset when playing in winds. It enables you to get additional distance and more accuracy for it does not drift off line as easily as a higher shot.

PLATE 79—*Downswing*

HITTING AN INTENTIONAL SLICE

At times you may find that you cannot surmount an obstacle by going either over or under it. If so, the only way to reach your objective efficiently is to go around it—to the right or left.

PLATE 80—*Slicing Around an Obstacle*—In the situation pictured in Plate 80 I find a tree between myself and the green which is my objective. I am so close I would have to use a short iron to get over the tree, thereby sacrificing distance. If I hit the ball straight out to the left past the tree, I will be in deep rough or woods. The solution is to curve the ball to the right around the tree.

The first step in playing a deliberate slice (flight of ball curves to the right) is to take an *open stance*.

The ball will be played approximately off the center of my stance.

Take the clubhead back *outside* the intended line of flight. This actually means pushing away from your body with your hands on the backswing.

Hands and club are quite high at the top of the backswing.

From this position at the top of the swing, pull down and across the ball (from outside the line of flight to inside) toward your left foot.

Keep the face of the clubhead slightly open at all times. Be careful that the clubhead does not turn over at any stage of the downswing and follow-through. You *must follow through*.

The curved flight of the ball is caused by the spin imparted as the clubhead cuts across the ball at an angle.

PLATE 80—*Slicing Around an Obstacle*

HITTING AN INTENTIONAL HOOK

PLATE 81—*Hooking Around an Obstacle*—This time I find it necessary to curve around this tree to the left if I am to drop the ball on the green in the distance.

To play the desired hook (curve to the left) I must first assume a *closed* stance, as shown.

The ball is to be played from a point nearly opposite the *right* foot.

In starting your backswing, pivot the right hip away from the ball, bringing the clubhead sharply around as you take it back. This will result in a so-called "flat" swing, for you are deviating from the usual upright swing.

Employ a normally full backswing.

Start the clubhead down by turning your body back to its original position, allowing the left arm and side to pull the clubhead.

Swing the clubhead out away from the body, allowing your wrists and the clubhead to turn over (roll) at moment of impact.

You can regulate the amount of curve by the degree to which you close your stance, and the flatness of your swing. In other words—for a sharp hook, use a pronouncedly closed stance and flat swing; for a slight hook, barely open the stance and flatten your swing very little.

It is important that you remember, in playing these shots, to keep your left arm straight throughout, and your head still.

Always follow completely through.

PLATE 81—*Hooking Around an Obstacle*

PLAYING FROM AN UPHILL LIE

PLATE 82—*Stance and Technique*—In the situation pictured here I am playing the ball from an uphill lie, with my right foot downhill from my left foot.

The ball is to be played from a point approximately off the center of my stance.

The weight is kept on the right foot, which is a natural tendency in this position.

The nature of the lie from which you are shooting is such that you will be hitting up on the ball and thus getting exaggerated height in the flight of the ball. For this reason you must use a longer club than you would use to get the same distance off a level lie.

The extra height is accounted for as follows: Your right foot being lower than your left, it is impossible for you to shift your weight on to the left foot properly at the time of impact. This situation causes you to *pull* the shot to the left, so you must make allowances by aiming to the right.

We remind you again—any time the weight is on the right foot at the time of clubhead impact with the ball, the flight of the ball will be abnormally high.

PLATE 82—*Stance and Technique*

PLAYING FROM A DOWNHILL LIE

PLATE 83—*Stance and Technique*—As pictured here, I am about to play the ball from a downhill lie, with my left foot several inches lower than my right.

The ball is approximately opposite a point nearly back to my right heel.

The stance is open.

The weight is principally on my left foot. This means that the tendency will be to hit down on the ball, causing the ball to take off on a low trajectory. Because of this, you should use a club with a more lofted face than you would select to get the same distance from a level lie.

Remember—any time you have more weight than usual on your left foot at the time of clubhead impact with the ball, the ball will travel abnormally low.

In executing the backswing, you should have the feeling that you are taking the clubhead practically straight up. The low sweep at the start of the backswing is very limited. Of course, if you exaggerate too much, you chop at the ball. Your principal concern is to avoid hitting the ground behind the ball.

Because the position of the left foot below the right is conducive to *hooking,* make allowances by aiming somewhat to the right.

PLATE 83—*Stance and Technique*

PLAYING FROM POSITION BELOW FEET

PLATE 84—*Stance and Execution*—As pictured in Plate 84, the ball is downhill from me, several inches below my feet which are level with each other.

This is one of the most difficult shots encountered, for you must reach abnormally for the ball. To offset this, be sure you stand closer than usual to the ball.

Play the ball from a point opposite the center of the stance. Keep your hands well ahead of the clubhead.

Use a longer club than you normally would for the desired distance. The reason—because you are standing above the ball you will not have the free body turn you usually employ. This means loss of distance.

Grip the club just as far up on the shaft as you can.

Always allow a little for a slice (curved flight to the right) because the lack of body-turn creates this tendency.

PLATE 84—*Stance and Execution*

PLAYING FROM POSITION ABOVE FEET

PLATE 85—*Stance and Execution*—In the situation pictured here I am standing below the ball. The ball is several inches above my feet.

I have *shortened my grip* on the club a distance approximately equal to the difference between the levels of the ball and my feet.

The ball is opposite a point nearer the *right* foot than usual. The stance is slightly open.

You must try to keep the club on as much of a straight line as possible in taking it back. The reason—to offset the tendency to swing in too flat an arc and consequently hook the ball too much. You cannot entirely eliminate the hook when you play a shot while standing below the ball, so make an allowance for it.

Keep a *firm grip* on the club. Be especially careful *not to let your wrists turn over (roll) with the club*. As a safeguard, keep the back of the left hand facing your objective as you swing into and through the ball.

Keep your head as still as possible.

Take a club longer than you would normally employ from a flat lie, for in gripping shorter, you automatically cut down the length of flight. If you try to offset this by hitting the ball harder, you will flatten the arc of your swing, and proportionately increase the sharpness of your hook.

PLATE 85—*Stance and Execution*

Byron Nelson (left) accepts the congratulations of Mike Turnesa as they walk off the 18th green at Moraine Country club, Dayton, Ohio, after second-round match in 1945 P.G.A. national tournament. Nelson, two down with four to go, shot birdie, birdie, eagle, par to win, 1 up. He then went on to take the championship.